❋ CONTENTS ❋

THE LANGUAGE OF PLANTS

UNDERSTANDING HOW PLANTS COMMUNICATE

Helena Haraštová
Darya Beklemesheva

ALBATROS

PLANTS ARE LIVING ORGANISMS

The plant kingdom resembles our world in many ways

OUR VERY STRANGE RELATIVES

Imagine a creature that breathes (even though it has no lungs), digests food (even though it has no stomach or intestines), excretes harmful substances from its body (even though it has no liver), responds to light and sounds (even though it has no eyes or ears), and even behaves intelligently (even though it has no brain). You know these creatures better than you think. That's because they're plants! We have so much in common with plants. In fact, we even have a common origin and ancestor. We are all living creatures.

LIFE-GIVING COOPERATION

ONCE UPON A TIME (2 TO 3 BILLION YEARS AGO)

Only unicellular organisms (similar to bacteria, protozoa, or cyanobacteria) lived on Earth.

Hello!

LATER

When you're successful, others imitate you. More and more complex organisms, composed of more and more cells, began to emerge and thrive.

Come and join us! We have lots of nutrients and work for everyone.

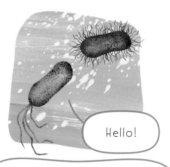

Haven't we met somewhere before?

FINALLY

Animals, plants, and fungi have become so different that you'd never guess that they had common origins.

I don't think I've had the pleasure.

HALF A BILLION YEARS AGO

Two unicellular organisms discovered that when they combined, they were stronger and more resilient!

What about working together?

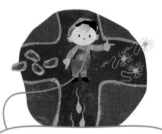

Let's do it!

EVEN LATER

The cells of each particular organism gradually specialized, depending on where it lived and what it needed for its life. Various types of cells emerged.

Nerve cells to the right, blood cells to the left, and sex cells straight ahead!

AND INSIDE . . .

If you look at a plant and an animal cell under a microscope, you'll see that they are a little different today.

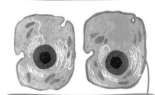

Don't we look good!

BEING A PLANT IS FAR FROM BORING

We now know of around 400,000 species of plant. But of course, it's not that easy to find new species, because, as we all know, plants don't just turn up and announce themselves to the botanist, and they don't leave tracks. Plants are unable to move to a better place to escape pests or to avoid drought, the heat, or the cold. However, they are capable of doing fascinating things—things that we have only recently begun to discover, thanks to modern technologies.

SOME PLANTS HAVE DISCOVERED A SPECIAL MEANS OF TRANSPORT, THOUGH—THEY KNOW HOW TO MAKE THEIR SEEDS TRAVEL LONG DISTANCES. ONE SUCH EXAMPLE IS THE CRAMBE TATARIA, A PLANT THAT WAITS UNTIL ITS SEEDS ARE READY THEN WITHERS COMPLETELY AND BREAKS OFF. THEN IT SIMPLY LETS THE WIND TAKE IT SOMEWHERE. AND WHILE FLYING IN THE AIR, IT DROPS ITS SEEDS TO THE GROUND.

Given that plants are stuck in one place their whole lives, they have had to develop some **sophisticated strategies** to:

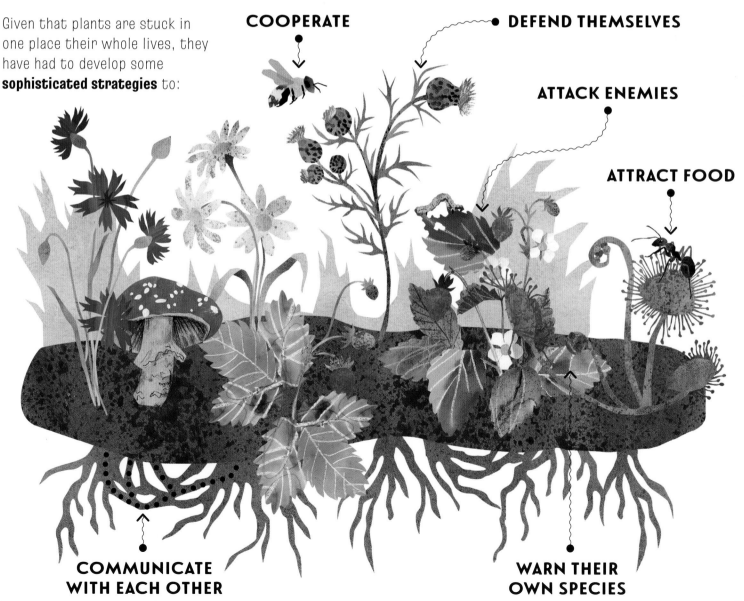

COOPERATE

DEFEND THEMSELVES

ATTACK ENEMIES

ATTRACT FOOD

COMMUNICATE WITH EACH OTHER

WARN THEIR OWN SPECIES

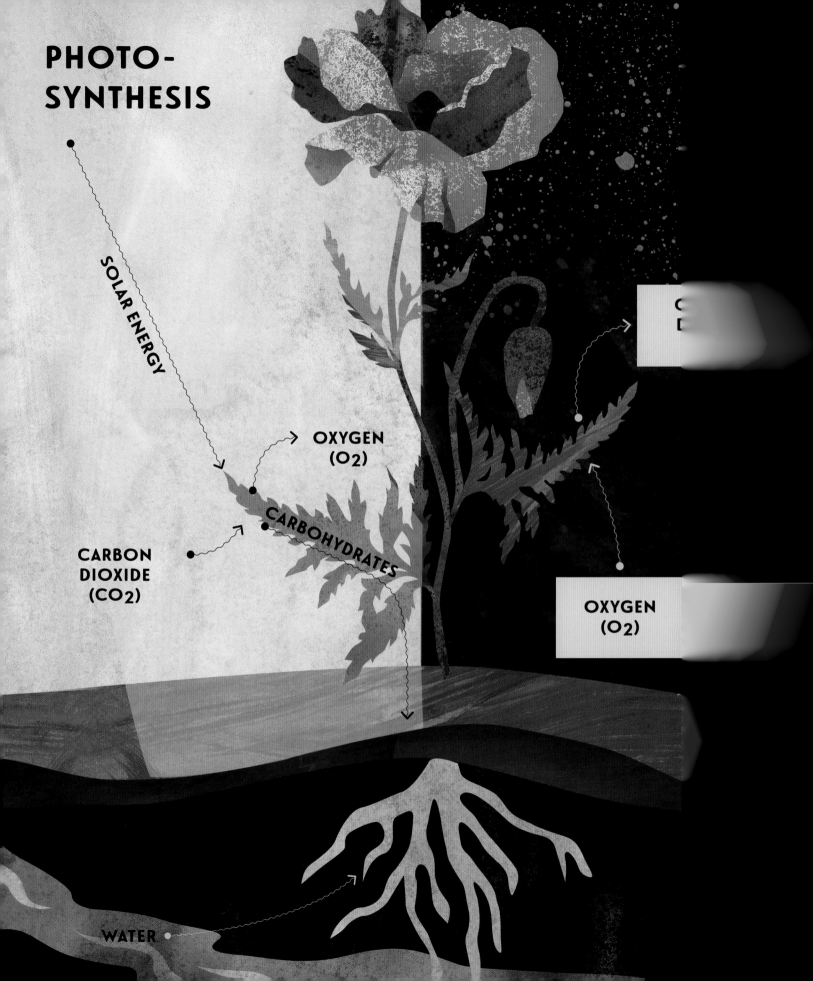

SOMETHING OUT OF NOTHING

Plants possess one incredible ability: they can make something out of nothing! Sounds like magic, doesn't it? The "nothing" that they make "something" from is, in fact, energy from the sun, air, and water. And the "something" they make is food. Plants make food not only for themselves, but also for all of us. Whether we eat vegetables, meat, or grains, all nutrients on Earth have their origins in plants. And remember, a byproduct of this production is the very oxygen we breathe. The process by which a plant performs this miracle is called **photosynthesis**.

WHAT ABOUT NIGHTTIME? PHOTOSYNTHESIS DOESN'T WORK AT NIGHT. INSTEAD, PLANTS BREATHE LIKE WE DO—THEY ABSORB OXYGEN AND RELEASE CARBON DIOXIDE. BUT THEY PRODUCE SUCH A TREMENDOUS AMOUNT OF OXYGEN DURING THE DAY THAT THERE'S ALWAYS ENOUGH LEFT OVER FOR US.

LEAVES ARE ESSENTIAL

The green leaves of plants are the secret of the whole process of photosynthesis. Their cells contain **chloroplasts**, in which there are chlorophyll pigments.

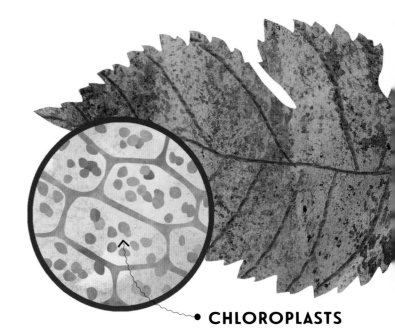

CHLOROPLASTS

Chlorophyll gives plants their green color. It also absorbs energy from the sun and turns it into carbohydrates. Without chlorophyll, photosynthesis would not be possible.

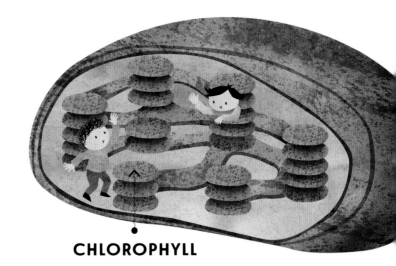

CHLOROPHYLL

HOW A FOREST BREATHES
If you stared at a tree at night, you would
notice that it slightly stoops its branches.
It relaxes in a way similar to we humans releasing
our muscles or slowing down the beatings
of our hearts during sleep.

BREATHING IN WINTER

In wintertime, plants go into hibernation, thereby reducing their need for oxygen to breathe. They don't die of asphyxiation, even though they only produce a minimal amount of oxygen. And why is it that we humans don't suffer from a lack of oxygen during the winter? Well, air circulates around the planet, so we're able to breathe oxygen produced, for example, by the coniferous forests of the taiga or by plants in the tropical rainforest!

A WORLD WITHOUT PLANTS?

We can't take it for granted that we live on a planet with enough oxygen and food, and with a safe environment for us to live in. We owe all of this to plants! However, plants become ill when people recklessly use harmful substances in agriculture and industry or they don't care about nature. Why not become a defender of plants? Why not look after the plants in your area?

"WOOD" WIDE WEB

Plants communicate with each other through their roots

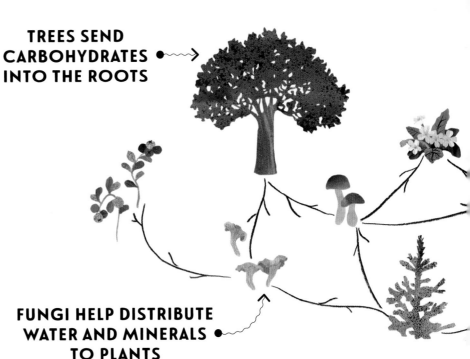

TREES SEND CARBOHYDRATES INTO THE ROOTS

FUNGI HELP DISTRIBUTE WATER AND MINERALS TO PLANTS

WHAT ARE ROOTS FOR?

For ages, people thought that plants needed roots just for stability and for drawing water and nutrients from the soil. But in the 1980s, scientists took a look underground and noticed that the roots of plants and fungi were interconnected. Why? It turned out that these connections were dense, ingeniously formed networks. Scientists began to call them **mycorrhiza**.

HOW DOES IT WORK?

The mycelium extends its fungal threads in different directions until it encounters the roots of plants. As soon as this happens, the two root systems connect and the fungi and plants become literally inseparable friends. To their allies, the fungi send water and minerals, which help the plants grow faster. The plants supply the fungi with carbohydrates that they cannot make themselves but which they cannot live without. It is no wonder that 70 to 90 percent of all plants and practically all fungi are hooked up to mycorrhiza. This system works in temperate woods, tropical rainforests, and even in the Arctic.

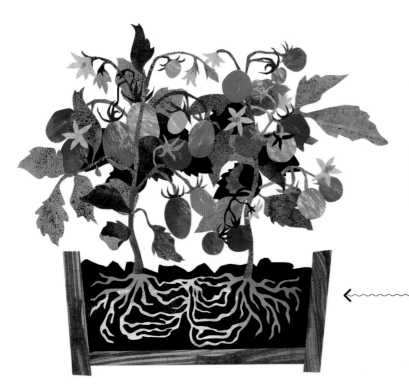

YOU CAN MAKE YOUR OWN MYCORRHIZAE ON A BALCONY. ALL YOU HAVE TO DO IS GET SOME SOIL WITH MYCORRHIZAL FUNGI IN IT (YOU CAN FIND THIS AT ANY GOOD GARDEN CENTER).

"WOOD" WIDE WEB

Scientists have found that a dense network of roots where fungi are present also connects individual plants to each other. Through mycorrhiza, they can help each other. Imagine the whole network as the branched-out brain of a forest, with many centers. Here, important information is stored in and sent from. Think of it as being like the internet, a worldwide network of interconnected computers we call the "world-wide web." This natural network has thus been given a similar nickname—the "**wood-wide web**."

1. Fungi. We are the messengers. We pass on nutrients, water, and information.

2. Old plants. We are the Founding Fathers of the network. Together with fungi, we form its information nodes.

3. Young plants. We're keen to join you, as soon as our roots are more developed.

4. Mother plant. I send nutrients to my seedlings so that they will grow well and prosper.

5. Seedling. Thanks to the nutrients from my mother plant, I grow stronger and thrive.

6. Auxin. You will find me in the roots of plants. I decide the direction they grow in.

7. Mycelium. We thin fungal threads form a dense and tremendously long network. You will find many miles of us in a mere teaspoon of soil!

8. Root. I am able to perceive the Earth's gravity, so I always grow toward the center of the earth. I look for water and nutrients for the plant and fix it firmly in the soil.

A MYSTERY LIKE A DETECTIVE STORY

What about cooperation between different species of plant? Scientists had long suspected that, through mycorrhiza, the birch tree and the fir tree had a mysterious alliance—that the birch sent nutrients to the fir in summer and the fir did the same for the birch in winter. So, they ran an experiment. In a group of birch trees, fir trees, and thuja trees, they randomly covered some of the plants with black bags, and therefore such trees were unable to perform photosynthesis. They also added extra radioactive carbon to some of the uncovered trees (plants can produce carbon through photosynthesis). When they later examined which trees contained radioactive carbon, surprisingly, it was present in some of the covered trees. But these trees could not produce any carbon, so they had clearly received a gift of carbon from plants that had more of it than they needed.

TREES COVERED WITH A BLACK BAG*

RADIOACTIVE CARBON

***COVERED TREES CANNOT PERFORM PHOTOSYNTHESIS**

WHEN THE WOOD-WIDE WEB IS BENEFICIAL

A NETWORK OF MUTUAL ASSISTANCE

Solidarity is common among plants. They most often share with each other carbon, nitrogen, phosphorus, and various hormones.

AN EARLY-WARNING NETWORK

Pests, drought, or fire? Plants give timely warnings to their neighbors in danger.

DONATE AND DIE

With the last of their strength, very old and dying trees pass on their nutrients to the young plants around them.

. . . AND THE OTHER SIDE OF THE "WEB"

THUJA

Remember the experiment with birch, fir, and thuja trees? It turned out that the thuja trees didn't get involved in helping their neighbors. They behaved as if they were not part of the experiment.

ORCHID

This plant willingly engages in mycorrhiza, but while others donate, the orchid only takes.

WALNUT TREE

The substances it sends to its plant neighbors weaken and kill them. It can't stand any competition.

MIGHTY SCENTS

Plants call for help and warn each other

HOW THE UNASSUMING ACACIA CAN KILL AN ANTELOPE

In the 1990s, conservationists in South African wildlife reserves were taken aback by the extraordinarily large numbers of dead kudu antelopes. The cause of the deaths of so many animals left them scratching their heads.

However, the veterinarians gradually ruled out all these possibilities and eventually identified the least likely perpetrator as the killer—**acacia trees**! But how did this actually happen?

A prime source of food for kudu antelopes has always been acacia leaves. The acacia defends itself against its herbivore aggressor by increasing the concentration of tannins in its leaves. Consequently, the leaves soon become bitter. So after a few mouthfuls, the antelopes move on to places where the leaves are still beautifully sweet. But that just isn't an option when the reserve is enclosed by a high fence. The antelopes' food sources were limited, and the acacia trees became in danger of being wiped out. That's why they began to warn each other. The trees under attack released a strong-smelling gas called ethylene into the air, which other acacias in the area detected. As a precaution, they also increased the concentration of tannins in their leaves. When the kudu antelopes eventually arrived, they were greeted with a hefty dose of poison.

SCENTS AS A WARNING

The story of the unfortunate antelopes—and the cleverly communicating plants—had an interesting outcome. Over time, the animals came to understand that on their expeditions to their beloved acacias, they would be safe if they approached the plants upwind. The ethylene warning only travels where the wind blows, so plants upwind from the hungry animals have no prior warning of their approaching. At the same time, antelopes no longer eat too many leaves from a single tree, but just nibble a few, so that the acacia does not have to defend itself with its full armory of tannins. In the end, nature restored its lost balance.

It might come as a surprise that trees that have not been attacked also pass on warnings by means of scent. Researchers verified this in an experiment in which they slightly damaged the leaves of a number of poplar and maple trees. The damaged trees began to emit phenolic compounds as a warning, and the scientists also detected the same compounds on trees in the area that were intact and undamaged! Now you can easily decipher the meaning of the pleasant scent of freshly cut grass—in fact, it is a call for help.

12

UGH, A CATERPILLAR!

Some plants can give a timely warning of the approach of caterpillars too.

Now there's a juicy leaf. *Yummy!* And then I'll have that one, and that one, and that one.

Hey, I'm not a piece of lettuce for your lunch! I can't save myself, but I can protect my cousins.

What's that? A caterpillar, you say? He won't like the taste of me!

WARNING SCENT

Ugh, how can such a beautiful leaf be so bitter? I'm off. I don't feel well.

BITTER SUBSTANCE

SCENTS AS A CALL FOR HELP

"SOS! Raise the alarm! There are plants infested with aphids, voracious beasts that are unaffected by plants' poisonous substances!" Sometimes plants are unable to get rid of the enemy by themselves, so they need someone's help. Over the course of time, plants have learned another clever trick with scents: by means of a special enticing scent, they can attract insects that have their own way of dealing with aphids, namely hoverflies.

Ouch, you got me! I'm dying!

THE HOVERFLY LAYS ITS EGGS IN APHIDS

IT'S ALL ABOUT ESSENTIAL OILS

Essential oils are various fragrant substances that plants make themselves. It is the oils that give the plants their smell. Some plants, such as pine, spruce, mint, and chamomile, produce large amounts of essential oils, and for humans, their scent is a defining characteristic. Some oils might have healing properties—science is still on the fence—while others are irritating or even harmful for humans.

One, two, three, four, halt! Our army will win! Hooray!

APHIDS ON RASPBERRIES

A HOVERFLY IS A SMALL INSECT THAT HAS A STRIPED COAT SIMILAR TO THAT OF A WASP. INSTEAD OF A STING, IT HAS AN OVIPOSITOR: A LONG SPIKED TUBE USED FOR LAYING EGGS DIRECTLY INTO THE APHIDS, THEREBY KILLING THEM.

HOW DOES A PLANT KNOW THAT IT IS UNDER ATTACK?

For humans and animals, it's easy: we have a brain and an interconnected nervous system, so when something injures us, the cells of our nervous system begin transmitting information about the threat at lightning speed. The information thus travels from the site of the injury to the central decision-making organ, namely the brain.

INFORMATION TRAVELS THROUGH THE NERVOUS SYSTEM FROM THE HURT SPOT TO THE BRAIN

However, plants have neither brains nor nerve cells, which presents a bit of a problem. It's still somewhat of a mystery how a plant as a whole realizes that it has been attacked on a certain part of its body. Plants probably use their sap vascular system, which can transmit electrical signals, to spread this information.

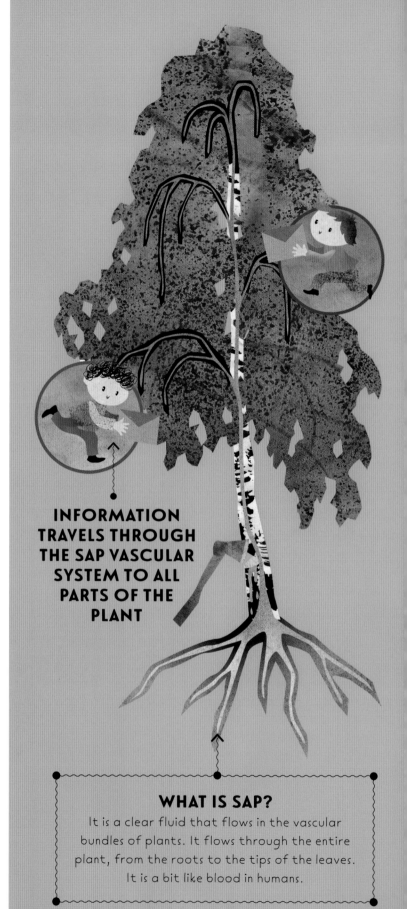

INFORMATION TRAVELS THROUGH THE SAP VASCULAR SYSTEM TO ALL PARTS OF THE PLANT

WHAT IS SAP?
It is a clear fluid that flows in the vascular bundles of plants. It flows through the entire plant, from the roots to the tips of the leaves. It is a bit like blood in humans.

LIFE-OR-DEATH STRUGGLE

Plants compete with one another

Children as well as adults sometimes butt heads. And it's the same with animals, which compete with each other for the most desirable female, or for breadcrumbs on the pavement. So what about plants? Are they unselfish, altruistic, always willing to lend a hand? Don't you believe it! Even plants compete with each other.

A FALSE UTOPIA

Imagine soil where individual plants are growing side by side in peace and harmony. They have enough:

1. **SUNLIGHT**
2. **SPACE**
3. **NUTRIENTS**
4. **WATER**

You will never find this kind of situation in nature. All plants need light, water, nutrients, and space to live, so of course they all strive for the biggest possible share of them! And when the amount of resources is limited, so begins a merciless struggle for the survival of the fittest.

RIVALRY—AN INGENIOUS TOOL OF EVOLUTION

Who wins? Well, it could be the one that has the most colorful and interesting flowers, thereby attracting the most pollinators.

Or it could be the one that grows the longest roots so that it is the quickest to reach water hidden beneath the surface.

Some carnivorous plants have learned to catch insects because they lived in nutrient-poor environments such as bogs. In order to have a richer diet than their competitors, they simply found a new way of living.

THE STRUGGLE FOR CONTROL OF THE SPACE

Research has shown that, as with humans and animals, individuals of the same plant species also compete. Researchers have noticed that some species of plant, such as oak trees, really like competing with one another. In deciduous forests, we can see a special kind of military offensive: the oaks try to outgrow other trees and each other, to extend their roots so that the others don't access their nutrients, and to raise more seedlings than their neighbors. In short, they try to control the whole area.

THE STRUGGLE FOR WATER AND NUTRIENTS

We already know that for proper growth and development, plants need a range of important nutrients that they get from the soil, and of course, enough water. Subtle battles are fought for both of these resources, and again, it's usually the one with an original solution who wins.

1. Peach and walnut trees, even beautiful sunflowers, release toxic substances (such as the juglone toxin) into the soil around them to drive away competitors.

Ha! Now you are mine, nutrients. All mine!

You can't call this good neighborly relations!

2. Other plants rely on the length of their roots, which they spread in an effort to take up as much space in the soil as quickly as they can.

3. Long roots also more quickly reach water sources that are deeper down in the soil.

Where's that water?

You don't need to have the longest roots. You just need to have them everywhere.

4. Spreading roots are good for catching rainwater.

5. In places where most plants would wither, those that need little water and nutrients prevail.

Isn't it lovely here?

THE STRUGGLE FOR LIGHT

Without light, plants would be unable to perform photosynthesis or process nutrients and they would die. They receive just two out of the three parts that the light consists of: the red and the blue parts. Plants don't absorb the green part, and so this light is reflected away from them—and that is why we see plants as green.

There is an old proverb that the sun shines the same on everyone. But plants would tell you this is utter nonsense! Although it might not seem so at first sight, plants have to fight actively for the life-giving rays of the sun.

Plants' access to the sun's rays varies during the day, not only according to how cloudy it is, but also according to the composition of the vegetation.

Kapok tree (1)
Plants naturally try to grow taller than the others in order to get as close as possible to the source of light. In doing so, they overshadow their competitors.

Cocoa tree (2) and coffee tree (3)
Plants that are unable to find their way to a sufficient amount of light grow smaller and weaker.

Bougainvillea liana plant (4)
The competition for light between the shoots and the young plants is tremendous! Only the most active will prevail.

Ferns (5)
Some plants have learned to emerge victoriously from the competitive struggle for light by means of an original solution: they fell in love with shade.

Rafflesia (6)
Parasites like rafflesia, a plant with enormous blooms, sponge on lianas, getting all necessary nutrients from them.

Eucalyptus
But too much light can harm plants. Many have learned to survive in the sun by turning away their leaves or their whole stem, so as not to be exposed to too much sunlight. As a result, they can thrive where other plants can't survive.

19

NO STRESS

Plants fear danger . . . and protect themselves

Have you ever had to deal with stress? It's not much fun. When a person is under too much pressure, the poor soul can't cope and their well-being suffers. Under stress, the human brain resorts to instinctive survival measures.

HOW DO PLANTS COPE WITH STRESS?

Throughout their lives, plants will encounter lots of stressful situations too. However, they have learned a unique ability that even humans don't possess: they trigger different responses depending on the kind of stress they have to deal with.

DROUGHT
The plant gives a command to close the pores of its leaves, through which it normally excretes water. The plant's roots are also coated with a waxy layer, which prevents water from escaping into the soil.

COLD
In annual plants that don't survive the freezing winter conditions, all the decisions conform to the necessity to create enough seeds that will survive in the soil until the spring. Even though the plant itself freezes to death, its offspring grows again.

PESTS
A special hormone activates the production of fragrant substances, which act as a warning to the surrounding plants or which attract creatures that eat pests.

POOR SOIL
Special substances suppress growth and development, which means that the plant is smaller and saves as much energy as it can.

MOLD
A special hormone stimulates the production of an acid that counteracts the mold.

WHEN THE STRESS IS TOO MUCH TO BEAR

But plants can only use their superpowers for stress that occurs over a short time period or at regular intervals. When they are subject to stress for a longer period, they may learn to live happily in unfavorable conditions by adapting. More often, though, we see signs of their discomfort.

- **THE PLANT GROWS SLOWLY OR NOT AT ALL**
- **IT IS WEAK AND DAMAGED**
- **IT DOES NOT REPRODUCE WELL**
- **IT BEARS FEW FLOWERS OR FRUIT**
- **IT CAN'T TRANSFER WATER AND NUTRIENTS EFFECTIVELY TO ALL PARTS OF THE PLANT**

HOW TO AVOID STRESS

1) Eat healthy. Focus on proper nutrients.

2) Live in a friendly environment. The soil needs to have the right composition.

3) Get to the root of the problem. In a stressed plant the root is weak and short.

THE BIG QUESTION

Do plants feel pain? We don't really need to worry about this. Plants react to stress, such as when you pluck a leaf or forget to water them, but they don't feel pain as we understand it. When in possible danger, they make an ultrasonic sound—but don't mistake this for the desperate cry of a tormented plant. It's just passing on the information: "This has just happened to me—watch out!"

MYSTERIOUS MEMORY

Plants remember things, although we don't fully understand how they do it.

You remember the cornflower that bragged all the time last year?

Yeah, I've heard she dried up completely!

LEARNING FROM EXPERIENCE

The memory processes of plants work differently than those of humans. They don't store memories as we know them (or, at least, we don't know that they do). They can't remember what they did yesterday and they haven't the foggiest idea about the things they liked when they were just little seeds. But, even so, they can learn from their experience, which means they remember which reactions worked well for them and which had no effect or were even harmful.

HOW PLANTS ADAPT THEIR REACTIONS

Plants can retain the memory of an effective reaction for quite a long time—up to 40 days. Scientists discovered this in experiments with a touch-me-not plant. This is a lovely tropical plant, with pretty purple flowers, that instantly closes its tiny leaves at the slightest touch or movement. In a 40-day study of the plant's reactions, researchers abruptly and repeatedly lifted the pot in which the touch-me-not plant was growing and observed the plant's behavior. At first, every time they lifted the pot, all the plant's leaves closed at once. However, as this action was repeated every day, the reactions of the plant eased off and became less and less noticeable . . . until one day, the plant stopped closing its leaves altogether. That's because it remembered that this action presented no danger.

22

LIGHT . . . WIND . . . LIGHT . . . WIND . . . JUST WIND?

In 2016, Australian researchers conducted an experiment with peas. They first placed a source of blue light alongside the plants and then waited for the peas to instinctively turn toward the light. After that, they pointed a small fan, as well as a light source, towards the plants. Finally, they directed the fan towards the plants, but without the light. The plants began to turn towards the fan, because they assumed that where there's a breeze, there's also light.

MEMORIES ARE NOT ALIKE

So, what actually was it that the plants remembered? Most likely, it wasn't the event itself, but just the reaction that brought them a reward. That's how they "knew" that it would benefit them to turn towards the source of the breeze, although they probably had no idea that there were people in white coats pointing an ordinary fan and blue lamp at them yesterday and the day before. However, the consciousness of plants is still a big mystery to us.

INHERITED MEMORY

Plants can store the memory of experience for a long time, and it seems they can even pass it on from generation to generation. Interestingly, we still have no idea how they do it. For example, not long ago, some areas of Canada were afflicted by severe drought. Scientists found that plants had survived in those places that had suffered a severe drought 20 years earlier. In areas of the country that had not experienced drought recently, the plants tended not to survive.

SENSES THAT WILL TAKE YOUR BREATH AWAY

Plants can sense
all beauties of the world

IT DOESN'T MAKE ANY SENSE!

Plants don't need classic sense organs to perceive light, sounds, or touches. Over the millions of years of their development, they've learned, in their own way, to see, hear, and touch the world. They take note of their surroundings with the aid of a wide variety of sensors—as many as 700 on one plant alone!

SIGHT

WHAT CAN THE PLANT "SEE"?

How do plants orient themselves and what of the things that humans see with their eyes do plants perceive?

An experiment with bean plants helped researchers study this question. Beans were planted in pots around a foot away from garden canes, which the plants like to wrap themselves around, because it allows them to grow upwards towards the sun.

1.

2.

SEEING WITH THE WHOLE BODY

If you were a plant, you would be concerned about the amount of light you were getting and the direction where the light was coming from. This is precisely what photoreceptors perceive. While humans have only 4 photoreceptors in their eyes, researchers have found 11 kinds of photoreceptors on a common plant such as the mouse-ear cress (*Arabidopsis thaliana*). There are photoreceptors all over a plant's body and so the plant perceives light through its leaves, stems, and branches.

SLOWNESS HAS THE POWER

In fact, you likely wouldn't notice with the naked eye how the beans were struggling for access to the cane and how purposefully they were trying to clamber up it. All plant movements are very, very slow. The researchers only recorded them by photographing the plants every 10 minutes and putting together a film from the resulting photographs.

Rubbish! It's speed that always leads to victory.

1. At first, the bean plants began lashing out their stems wildly and vigorously in all directions in search of the cane.
2. The dilemma for the plants was that there were more pots in the experiment than canes—so it was vitally important to be the first to find a cane!
3. As soon as a plant managed it, its behavior immediately changed. Instead of wild movements in all directions, it began to twine itself around the cane in a concentrated manner, to secure the best access to light.
4. The neighboring bean plant attempted to find another cane nearby, but soon realized that the effort was futile and gave up. The wild movements in all directions ceased, and the plant wilted sadly. It somehow "saw" that the other plant had won. How? We have no clue.

HEARING

WHAT IS SOUND?

In animals, hearing serves primarily to attract a partner, find food, and warn of an approaching enemy. But could it be possible that plants use it in a similar way? We now know that plants perceive sound waves through special receptors. They act as membranes. Sound isn't some kind of sorcery, but is rather just a series of sound waves moving in space. When a sound wave hits a membrane, it vibrates—which tells the plant something is going on. Sound receptors in plants are incredibly clever and they're certainly able to recognize the source of a sound and react to it.

AN INHERITED SUPERPOWER

Plants can match a specific sound to a specific situation due to genetic tools from their ancestors, their own memory, and their ability to store life experiences. We don't yet know how precisely they distinguish between individual types of sounds. But one thing is certain: they can definitely do it. When a hungry caterpillar shows up near a plant, the plant knows about it before the ravenous creature even takes a bite of the first leaf—it hears its movement and correctly deciphers it.

A PLANT FILLS ITS LEAVES WITH A PROTECTIVE CHEMICAL THAT DRIVES THE CATERPILLAR AWAY.

SOUNDS HELP US UNDERSTAND THE WORLD

Scientists recently confirmed this in two experiments, one in which watercress were played a sound recording of a crawling caterpillar. By contrast, in the second experiment, the sound of a bumblebee was played to pea plants. The peas immediately increased the amount of sugar in their nectar so as to give the bumblebee a sweet treat. Correctly identifying the source of a sound thus makes life easier for plants.

LET'S DANCE!

Although the conscious movements of plants towards light or some other necessity tend to be so slow that we're unable perceive them with the naked eye, there is one plant that can move to the beat! It's even been given the nickname "the dancing plant," although technically it's called *codariocalyx motorius*. People living in Southeast Asia, where this pretty thing comes from, know that if you clap rhythmically near "the dancing plant" or play your favorite music, its leaves will dance!

MOZART AND OTHERS

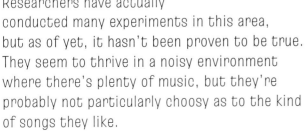

Many people believe that their houseplants prefer a certain type of music, such as Mozart. Researchers have actually conducted many experiments in this area, but as of yet, it hasn't been proven to be true. They seem to thrive in a noisy environment where there's plenty of music, but they're probably not particularly choosy as to the kind of songs they like.

THE MYSTERY OF SOUNDS

Plants not only receive sounds, but they also emit them. However, the frequency of such sounds is low, only 50 to 120 Hz, and they're not audible to the human ear. Nevertheless, special devices can easily record them. Plants make such sounds particularly when they're under stress, such as when they are exposed to drought, when we cut off their leaves, or when we overwater them. Did you know that:

Each of these sounds is specific. The surrounding plants probably know what is bothering their fellow plant.

Herbivores are familiar with the sounds of plants, because they feed on them and it's important for them to know what condition the plants are in.

Plant calls probably come from the woody vascular bundles of the plant.

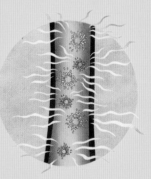

These sounds can travel a distance of up to 16 feet.

Will we ever be able to decipher plant sounds and find out exactly when a plant needs repotting or when it thirsts for water? Perhaps we're not far off from the time when we really will be able to communicate with plants.

SMELL

SOMETHING SMELLS GOOD!

We already know that plants can smell all kinds of scents. For example, plants attacked by insects send their plant comrades warning signals with volatile substances. But smell can also help them find food. It's almost as if tomato plants were made for the parasitic dodder plant. It loves to twine itself around them and then it cheekily feeds off them. As soon as it smells tomatoes, it begins growing with twisting movements in the direction of the smell until it finds the plant it seeks. The fact that the dodder is guided by "smell" and not "sight" has been confirmed by researchers, who presented the plant with various objects that they had given the scent of tomatoes. In each case, the dodder enthusiastically dashed towards the objects.

SO WHAT ABOUT THE NOSE, THEN?

A plant doesn't need anything like a human nose or an animal snout. Its whole body can perceive smells and odors. These are transmitted by small molecules. While humans and other animals, on the surface of their bodies, use "olfactory receptors"—bodily organs used for smelling—to pick up smells (for example, in their noses), in plants, odor molecules bind directly to the plant's cells and stimulate a reaction there. Although this process is rather slow, it is more than enough for a plant's survival. In any case, a plant couldn't run away from an awful stink, even if it wanted to.

TOUCH

PROTECTION

Some plants are particularly sensitive to touch: for example, the nettle defends itself from human fingers with stinging hairs, and the well-known touch-me-not plant folds up its leaves at the slightest stimulus, such as a gust of wind or the landing of an insect. These abilities help them survive.

CARNIVOROUS PLANTS

An example of a carnivorous plant that has devised a sophisticated way of catching insects is the Venus flytrap. It lures ants, spiders, flies, and wasps with sweet droplets of nectar that are secreted on the edges of the leaves that form the trap. The leaves also have very sensitive hairs, and the moment a hungry insect triggers at least two of them, the leaves snap shut as quick as a flash, trapping it inside with no hope of escape. With the help of digestive enzymes, it slowly savors its prey. Yummy for the plant, but yikes for the bug!

PLEASE SUPPORT ME

We most often see the use of touch with climbing plants. They grow quickly when they can cling to a surface or a pole that supports them as they move upwards. People often use them to cover unsightly walls or to beautify wooden fences. In this way, they've learned to help plants and use them to their benefit. But few people have an idea of how sensitive the touch of these climbing plants is. They can twist themselves around a wire only a fraction of a millimeter thin—so thin that human fingers would scarcely be able to feel it! However, the plants that have made the best use of their sense of touch are . . .

VENUS FLYTRAPS

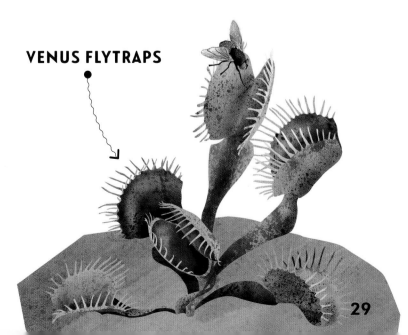

CLEVER POLLINATION

Plants can make themselves immortal

LET'S MULTIPLY

Like any living organism, plants want to have offspring. Over time, different groups of plants have developed ingenious ways of reproducing, from spores, rhizomes, and stolons to complex processes of sexual reproduction. For the male and female plant cells to come together, plants have learned to use **pollination**. Although some plants use wind or water to transfer pollen from one plant to another, many others have struck up mutually beneficial relationships with **pollinators**.

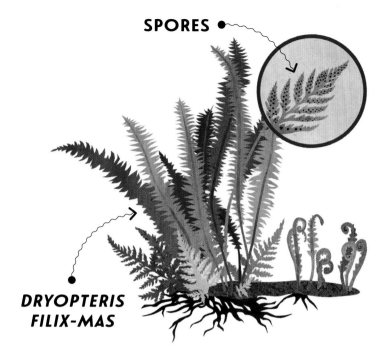

SPORES

DRYOPTERIS FILIX-MAS

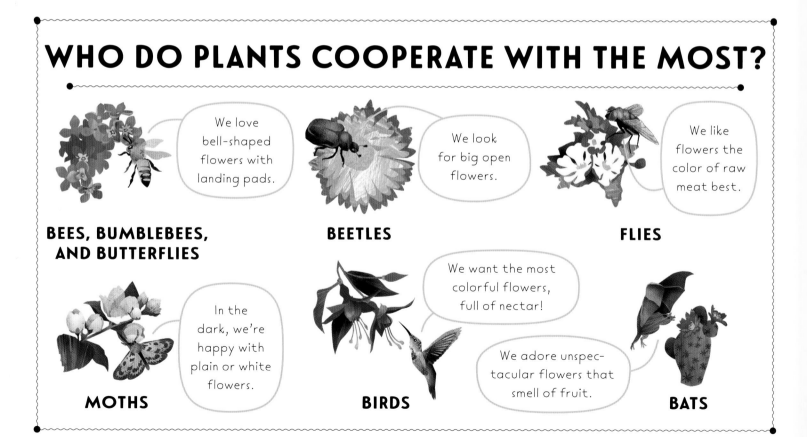

WHO DO PLANTS COOPERATE WITH THE MOST?

We love bell-shaped flowers with landing pads.

BEES, BUMBLEBEES, AND BUTTERFLIES

We look for big open flowers.

BEETLES

We like flowers the color of raw meat best.

FLIES

In the dark, we're happy with plain or white flowers.

MOTHS

We want the most colorful flowers, full of nectar!

BIRDS

We adore unspec-tacular flowers that smell of fruit.

BATS

We can add rodents, reptiles, and even monkeys to the list. In order for the plants to attract a suitable pollinator, they create strong scents at times when their pollinators are active (which means some flowers don't give off scents until the evening). They also use the extraordinary shapes and colors of their blooms, or interesting contrasts, to catch attention. But there's massive competition, so it pays to be original. For example, the mature dragon lily not only attracts flies with its flower's deep red color—it has also learned to create an odor that smells like rotting flesh! Flies land on its flowers thinking they'll be able to lay their eggs there, but this is another case of the plant being smarter than the animal.

So the next time you smell the intoxicating scent of meadow flowers, try to resist the temptation to pick a flower and take it home with you. Remember how cleverly plants have managed to cope with all the disadvantages of their place in nature. If you keep quiet, you might see an inquisitive little pollinator going towards the flower. *Shh!* Don't frighten it off.

WANT TO FIND OUT MORE?

Would you like to become a scientist and study plants and the fascinating ways they communicate? If so, here are a few things to read for starters:

GAGLIANO, Monica. *Thus Spoke the Plant.*

POLLAN, Michael. "The intelligent Plant." In the *New Yorker*, 2013.

WOHLLEBEN, Peter. *The Hidden Life of Trees.*

ZIEGE, Madlen. *Nature Is Never Silent.*

DK and Smithsonian Institution. Trees, Leaves, Flowers and Seeds: *A Visual Encyclopedia of the Plant Kingdom.*

www.livescience.com

www.nationalgeographic.com

Special thanks to Dr. Marie Kotasová Adámková from Masaryk University in Brno, Czechia, whose expertise and talent helped this book to be very accurate and yet comprehensible for young readers.

THE LANGUAGE OF PLANTS

UNDERSTANDING HOW PLANTS COMMUNICATE

© B4U Publishing for Albatros,
an imprint of Albatros Media Group, 2023
5. května 1746/22, Prague 4, Czech Republic

Written by Helena Haraštová
Illustrations © Darya Beklemesheva, c/o Advocate Art, 2022
Translated by Mark Worthington
Edited by Scott Alexander Jones

www.albatrosbooks.com

GLOSSARY

Auxin
A plant hormone that controls the extent
of the growth of roots and stems.

Carnivorous plants
Plants that get some of their nutrients from small
creatures that they can catch and kill, mostly insects.

Cell
The basic building block of living organisms.

Chlorophyll
A green pigment found in plants, cyanobacteria,
and some algae.

Chloroplasts
Organelles in plant cells that have the chlorophyll
pigment in them and perform photosynthesis.

Climbing plants
Plants that need to lean on rocks, trees, walls,
or other kinds of support.

Essential oils
Substances in plants that have various scents
and odors.

Ethylen
A colorless gas with a sweet smell.

Fungi
A very large separate group of organisms that
includes all kinds of species, from yeasts and molds to
mushrooms that grow in the forest. It is these forest
varieties that create very dense networks of roots
in the soil, through which the surrounding plants can
transmit information and nutrients.

Hormones
Chemical compounds in the bodies of all plants, animals,
and humans that transmit information between cells
and trigger various reactions.

Mycelium
A dense underground network of fungal threads.

Mycorrhiza
Friendly coexistence between fungi and plants (trees)
in which organisms communicate with each other via
the root system.

Nervous system
A network of interconnected cells in most animals and
in humans that transmit stimuli and reactions to them.

Nutrients
Substances that all living organisms need to absorb
in order to grow and survive.